CONTENTS

For Sadie, an unforgettable blending of warmth, wisdom and humor.

INTRODUCTION

Ethics are the moral principles we create to govern our behavior in the various spheres of our experience. They are an everpresent element in our day-to-day life. We speak of people as being ethical or unethical individuals. We set up standards of ethics in the fields of business, law, medicine and sports. We judge attitudes and actions by ethical criteria and we are frequently confronted by situations that demand an ethical definition and response.

Ethical principles express themselves as rules of conduct to which we subscribe and hold ourselves accountable. When we characterize a mode of behavior as right or wrong, we render an ethical judgment. Ethics take the form of specific instructions, rather than generalized or abstract ideas (giving to the poor and selling at a fair price, rather than compassion and honesty). And ethics focus upon concrete acts, rather than questions of being or belief (people are called ethical, not because of what they happen to be, but because of how they conduct themselves).

History is, at core, the story of our efforts to create and sustain workable social groupings. And ethics serve as the "glue" that holds these groups together. A society without religion may be, in the minds of religious believers, a society without hope, but it can function and survive. A society without social ideals may be a society without compassion, but it can function and survive. But a society without an ethical system, without a code of conduct which a majority of its members comprehend and are committed to uphold, stands in direct opposition to social order of any kind; it is a contradiction in terms.

A society's ethics grow out of its history, its cultural traditions, and its values. Embraced, as they must be, by the majority of its members, ethics afford a revealing view of that society's character. Jewish ethics have their origin in the Bible, Talmud, legend and folklore as well as in the lifestyles of Jewish communities and in the ideas of Jewish thinkers. They form a composite of Judaism's conception of moral life, transcending the boundaries of time and place.

And yet, it was not until the Middle Ages that Jewish ethical writings emerged as a distinct and independent body of literature. Although the Bible and Talmud contain a good deal of ethical content, the subject matter takes the form of unconnected insights and sayings, a random collection of ethical references, rather than an organized structure of thought. Only in the Middle Ages did there crystallize a literary form to explore ethical ideas in a systematic fashion, and to formulate a practical code of conduct based on these ideas.

From the Middle Ages on, ethical writings were produced in increasing number in the Jewish communities of Spain, Germany, France, and Eastern Europe. Eventually these came to be recognized as a distinct and independent branch of Hebrew literature (Sifrut haMusar). Although marked by a diversity of people, perspectives, and places, the various works share a number of defining similarities.

To begin with, Jewish ethical literature is practical. It deals with people in real-life situations. It focuses on the specific moral implications of an issue, and it translates its insights into the gritty idiom of human interaction. Ethical thinkers do not project remote theories, they prescribe approaches to living that are to be implemented here and now.

Then, too, ethical literature serves as an educational "middle-man" between those who comprise Judaism's intellectual advance-guard—the scholar, the philosopher—and the people at large. The ethical writer presents ideas in language that can be broadly and easily grasped, in terms that can be concretely applied, and at a pace that does not jar the rhythms or threaten the stability of communal life. This was particularly crucial given the uncertain and often dangerous circumstances that have confronted Diaspora Jewry. Thus, the philosopher may conceive a new interpretation of religious meaning and obligation which he imparts to the highly educated few. The ethical writer, on the other hand, works to communicate this new interpretation to the many, and to adapt it to the existing code of behavior.

The originality of Jewish ethical writing lies not only in what it says, but in how it says it. Jewish ethical writers have employed means of communication that would reach the greatest number of people in the most memorable manner. And they have invented a number of unique literary forms to say what they have wanted to say. These include the "classical" ethical works, monographs, homiletic literature, ethical wills and letters, eulogies, fables and poetry.

The excerpts in this book run the gamut of Jewish ethical thinking. They cover many issues, they use a variety of styles, and they come from many places. Much of this material has a contemporary ring. With minor modifications of reference and style, the material can be directly applied to issues and situations confronting us today. For in a world beset by barriers and divisions, ethics stand out as society's universal language.

FREE WILL
בחירה חפשית

SOURCES:

MISHNEH TORAH
COMMENTARY TO THE MISHNAH

AUTHOR:

Rabbi Moses Ben-Maimon
(1135–1204)

Widely known as Maimonides, Rabbi Moses Ben-Maimon is also referred to by the initials of his name - RaMBaM. Born in Spain to a family of scholars, he and his family fled from religious persecution, lived in Morocco for a time, emigrated to Eretz Yisrael, and finally settled in Egypt. Maimonides earned his living as a physician, serving as court doctor to the royal family of Saladin. Active in Jewish communal affairs, Maimonides was recognized as an authority on Jewish tradition throughout the Middle East. He produced a wealth of scholarly literature. After his death, Maimonides was honored by the saying "From Moses to Moses, there arose none like Moses."

Free will is granted to every man. If he wishes to direct himself toward the good way and become righteous, the will to do so is in his hand; and if he wishes to direct himself toward the bad way and become wicked, the will to do so is likewise in his hand. Thus it is written in the Torah, "Behold, the man is become as one of us, knowing good and evil" (Genesis 3:22) - that is to say, the human species has become unique in the world in that it can know of itself, by its own wit and reflection, what is good and what is evil, and in that it can do whatever it wishes...

Do not say in surprise, "How can a man do all that he desires and his actions be under his control? Can he do anything in the world without the permission and will of his Creator?..." Know that even though everything is done according to God's will, our actions remain under our control. How is this? In the same way that the Creator willed that all created things should have the tendency which He desired, so did He desire that a man should be possessed of free will, that all his actions should be under his control, and that there should not be anything to compel or withhold him, but that of his own accord and by the mind with which God had endowed him... For this reason is a man judged according to his own actions..."

YAD TESHUVAH V 1-4

It is impossible for man to be innately good or bad, just as it is impossible for him to be born skilled in a particular art. It is possible, however, for him to be susceptible from his very birth to the acquisition of good or bad characteristics. If one who has a good mind is left without instruction, he will without doubt remain ignorant. But on the other hand, if a dull, phlegmatic person is given instruction, he will gradually succeed in acquiring knowledge and understanding...

According to the Torah, man's conduct is entirely in his own hands... If he were compelled to act according to the decree of fate, he would have no freedom of choice, and the commands of the Torah would become null and void. It would also be useless for him to study... and his reward and punishment alike would be pure injustice...

The truth is, man has full command over all his actions... For this reason God tells him: I have set before you this day life and death, good and evil, therefore choose life!

MISHNAH COMMENTARY EIGHT
CHAPTER VIII

Maimonides states that every human being is endowed with free will. This is the essential foundation of all Jewish ethical thinking. Without it we could not talk about people being ethical or unethical, for there would be no freedom of choice.

Maimonides explains free will as it relates to ethics:

Each of us has the ability to recognize good and evil and to understand the difference between them.

Each of us has the opportunity to choose to live according to either righteous or wicked principles.

Each of us has the capacity to grow through good deeds. No one is born good or evil. These are learned patterns of behavior. We all have within ourselves the potential for improvement.

We are all personally responsible for our attitudes and actions.

Maimonides also deals with what may seem to be a puzzling contradiction in Judaism's teachings. On the one hand, God is the all-powerful, all-knowing Creator of the universe. On the other hand, we pos-sess free will and are, therefore, held strictly accountable for what we do. How can this be? May not wicked individuals justify their behavior by arguing that they are simply obeying the will of God?

Maimonides presents a more complex view of the work and will of the Creator. Granted that God created the universe. Granted too that everything in the universe is subject to God's will. However, would it not be within God's power to create a species - the human race - that is itself endowed with free will? What God has created, in other words, is not an end-product, but a dynamic process, an evolving world peopled by constantly developing human beings with freedom of choice and responsibility for the paths they choose.

When we deny personal responsibility, we barter away our freedom as well. Responsibility is a burden that liberates, enabling an individual to say, "I can make of my life what I choose. The responsibility rests with me—precisely where the possibilities begin."

STUDY QUESTIONS

1 What does Maimonides mean when he uses the term "free will?" Do you agree that every human being is granted free will? Can you back up your opinion with one or two specific examples from your own experience?

2 Why is free will considered essential to Jewish ethics? Why would the absence of freedom of choice make the commands of the Torah null and void?

3 While we may, indeed, have the ability to recognize the difference between good and evil, we are not born with that understanding. It is acquired through a process of learning and doing. What have been some of the important ways in which you have learned to distinguish between good and evil?

4 How do you think Maimonides might have replied to the following statements:

"That's the way the ball bounces!"

"It's human nature to be selfish and greedy."

"Don't curse the darkness; light a candle."

5 Maimonides proposes that each of us is a freely acting agent, and therefore responsible for our actions. On the other hand, he also teaches us that God knows all and controls all. What conflict, if any, exists between these two ideas? Does a belief in human free-will limit, in any way, a belief in God's omnipotence?

6 How do you explain the idea that free will and personal responsibility are intimately related to, and dependent upon, one another? Why, in your opinion, do people so often plead powerlessness in the face of responsibility? In what sense do we barter away our freedom when we avoid responsibility? Why do we say that responsibility is a burden that liberates?

7 Why are Maimonides' ideas about free will considered a message of optimism and hope?

8 Drawing from your own experiences, can you point to instances where freedom and responsibility have gone hand-in-hand?

9 There are those philosophers and thinkers who, trying to account for the existence of evil in this world, have proclaimed God to be "dead", or non-existent. How can evil exist in a world ruled over by a just and omnipotent God, they ask. How could a compassionate, all-powerful God allow the pain and suffering of an Auschwitz? What are your ideas and feelings on this issue? How do these difficult questions relate to the teachings of Maimonides?

FOR DISCUSSION

When he envisioned the creation of a Jewish State, Theodor Herzl, father of modern Zionism, declared: "If you will it, it is no dream." What do you think he meant? Discuss some of the ways in which the creation and history of the State of Israel express the free will and sense of responsibility of the Jewish people.

SPEECH
דבור

SOURCE:

HAFEZ HAYYIM

AUTHOR:

Israel Meir Ha-Kohen
(1838 – 1933)

Born in Poland, Israel Meir Ha-Kohen was widely revered by the Jews of Eastern Europe as a model of piety and saintliness. A Talmud scholar, he earned his living as a bookkeeper in a grocery store managed by his wife. So many students came to study with him that his home became a yeshivah. He wrote a variety of learned books to strengthen Jewish life. The most famous was Hafez Hayyim (He Who Desires Life). *This work was so popular and influential that Rabbi Ha-Kohen himself came to be known as the Hafez Hayyim.*

Those who listen to slanderous gossip are just as guilty as the talebearer. Repeated use of the evil tongue is like a silk thread made strong by hundreds of strands. The foul sin of talebearing often results in a chain of transgression.

Leprosy was regarded as a punishment for slander, because the two resemble each other: they are both slightly noticeable at the outset, and then develop into a chronic infectious disease. Furthermore, the slanderer separates husband from wife, brother from brother, and friend from friend; he is therefore afflicted with the disease which separates him from society . . .

If a person knows that someone has committed an injustice to his friend - perhaps cheated him or stolen from him or verbally fooled him - and he knows that the guilty person did not repay the theft or ask for forgiveness for his dishonesty, then the person who knows of these actions is permitted to tell others in order to help the injured party and protect others. But seven conditions must be present:

1. The person needs to have evidence of the dishonesty himself and not merely to have heard rumors about it.

2. The person must be very cautious and weigh the matter thoroughly to see whether it actually was a case of wrongdoing. And then he needs to think about it carefully before acting on his knowledge.

3. He must admonish the dishonest person privately in a quiet, reassuring manner to see whether he will change his ways. If not, he may speak out publicly.

4. He must not make the offense seem greater than it is.

5. He needs to examine his own motives and make sure he's not slandering the person because of a private grudge, but is doing so in good faith and for constructive reasons.

6. If there are any ways through which he can get around the situation without slandering the person, he should pursue those methods first.

7. As a result of his action, he must not bring greater punishment on the guilty person than a court might order if the person were to be tried in court.

In addition, the person who publicly maligns someone else must himself be honest and not guilty of the same crimes for which he is criticizing another... And he must be sure the people to whom he is speaking about the dishonesty are not evil people who indulge in the same practices themselves.

The spreading of gossip is viewed with a jaundiced eye in Jewish thinking. Judaism focuses upon neither the literal nor the legal aspects of the question, but rather upon the human elements involved.

In Jewish tradition, a good name is a uniquely precious possession, which must be rigorously protected both by the force of law and the canons of ethics.

Persons who listen to slanderous gossip are considered just as guilty as the talebearer. Gossip and slander, unlike such crimes as robbery and murder, cannot be committed in a vacuum; they require both a teller and a listener. Accordingly, those who choose to listen are more than merely witnesses to the act. They are accessories.

Moreover, listening lends legitimacy to the spreading of gossip and slander. It encourages others to become listeners or tellers and the talebearer to repeat the story again and again. There is no summoning it back; it will pass on, from person to person, from group to group, like "a silk thread made strong by hundreds of strands..."

The disease of gossip and slander attacks not only individuals but groups, and even entire nations and religions. Racial, religious and ethnic prejudices feed upon gossip and slander. Our own history offers a vast array of cases in point. Though the accusations made against our people may have been untrue, illogical, inconsistent and often bizarre, they have been believed and have been a major cause of Jewish suffering.

The necessary conditions set down by Rabbi Israel before speaking out against someone in public all affirm Judaism's profound reluctance to damage an individual's reputation, even when the damage may be deserved. Such a recourse must be regarded as a tactic of last resort. Speaking out against someone who has done wrong is defined not as a penalty, but only "in order to help the injured party and protect others."

Although speaking out in public is a strong act, only to be undertaken after much thought, neither may we remain silent if we can help right a wrong: "You shall not stand silent while your neighbor bleeds" says the Torah.

STUDY QUESTIONS

1 How are gossip, slander, and talebearing different from each other? How are they the same?

2 How can gossip, which can be thought of as merely frivolous speech, actually lead to harm?

3 Gossip has become a multi-million dollar industry. Gossip columnists defend their profession by claiming to "give the public what it wants". What do you think the public wants to know? Why are some people so eager to listen to intimate details of the private lives of famous people?

4 How do you think Rabbi Israel might have responded to the following arguments?

A. "I'm just relating it the way it actually happened. Why do you criticize me for telling the truth?"

B. "If they were so concerned about their reputations, why did they behave like that in the first place?"

C. "Freedom of speech, and of the press, are cornerstones of democracy. You must not muzzle the media. The public has a right to know!"

D. "He's a liar and a cheat. I have a moral duty to let people know with whom they are dealing!"

5 Does the popular expression, "Sticks and stones will break my bones, but names will never hurt me" have a place within the ethical system set forth by the Hafez Hayyim?

6 In what sense can gossip and slander be compared to such diseases as cancer and leprosy? Have you ever found yourself looking at someone in a different light after hearing a scandalous story about him or her?

7 In what circumstances, according to the Hafez Hayyim, are we allowed to do damage to the reputation of a person, a group of people, or a business? What steps must we take before speaking out? How do we know that Rabbi Israel viewed the (necessary) damage of a reputation not as a punishment in its own right but as a means of protection?

8 The rabbis taught "Let not a man dilate in praise of his neighbor, lest from his praise there is a passing to his blame." (Baba Batra 164b). Public praise can lead to individual jealousies, which in turn can lead to slander. Do you agree with the causative nature of this chain of events? Can you recall an instance in your own experience when excessive praise by a parent, teacher or friend has led to envy, and then to "blame" through gossip or slander?

FOR DISCUSSION

The Talmud states that most people cannot resist uttering slanderous remarks on a day to day basis (Baba Batra 164b). Does this observation reflect the social nature of your community environment? To what extent are gossip and slander an integral part of your community's makeup?

REPENTANCE

תשובה

SOURCE:

SHA'AREI TESHUVAH
(THE GATES OF REPENTANCE)

AUTHOR:

Jonah Ben-Abraham Gerondi
(1200 – 1263)

Born in Gerona, Spain, Jonah Ben-Abraham Gerondi gained fame as a rabbi, teacher, writer and moral thinker. He spoke out against what he saw as Spanish Jewry's disregard of the mitzvot, particularly those commandments dealing with people and their relations to one another. His ethical doctrine was based not on mystical speculation, but on halachah and aggadah. His comprehensive study of the process of repentance was done in the form of a monograph. The first major work of this kind in medieval Hebrew literature, it served as a model for subsequent ethical monographs. In the final years of his life, Gerondi, on the first stage of his journey to Eretz Yisrael, was convinced to remain in and serve the Jewish community of Toledo. He established a yeshivah in that city, and died shortly thereafter.

A person who has committed a sin, and who desires to enter the ways of repentance ... should proceed as follows:

In the same day, he should spurn all his former sins and pretend that he was born anew, so that he is free from all debits and credits. This day is the beginning of his career, when he lays out a good course for the future, a way that will bring him to perfect repentance. He should make himself feel that the potency of his old sins is gone, as if they had been physically thrown away.

He must not allow any guilt feelings to take hold of him, or to break his resolution by reminding him of his shameful past, when, like a thief, he transgressed again and again ... He should remember that this is the policy of the Creator, to keep His hand outstretched, in order to receive those who return.

The holiest day of the Jewish year, Yom Kippur (the Day of Atonement), celebrates neither an event of national significance, as do Passover and Hanukkah, nor an occasion of religious moment, as do Simhat Torah and Shavuot. Rather, Yom Kippur focuses upon the efforts of the individual to repent. Repentance is an act of highest priority in our tradition. As Rabbi Abbahu states in the Babylonian Talmud, "In the place where penitents stand, even the wholly righteous cannot stand."

Rabbi Gerondi presents his guiding principles of repentance, and sets forth a process by which it can best be realized. His concern is not so much the expiation of a particular sin, but rather the moral transformation of the sinner. The first paragraph of his text underscores this aim. Gerondi does not render the act of repentance mechanical and automatic. First, the person must desire to repent; it has to be a conscious decision, a matter of active choosing. And what is desired is not simply to repent a particular sin, but "to enter the ways of repentance," implying an overall redefinition of lifestyle and values.

Accordingly, "he should spurn all his former sins..." A transgression does not exist in a vacuum, but is part of a larger behavior pattern. "In the same day" teaches us that repentance must be spontaneous, not ritualized. It must grow out of self-awareness and honest resolve, and not because a particular ceremony of repentance happens to have come around. While the Ten Days of Penitence, beginning on Rosh Hashanah and culminating on Yom Kippur, mark a time of special penitential concentration, they represent an intensification of an ongoing process, not an act apart. We are not supposed to be repentant only on the ten prescribed days any more than we are supposed to live like free people only on Passover.

One may wonder if a person can just shake away the past and march into the future, morally untroubled by what went on before. Gerondi sometimes sounds more like a therapist than a teacher of ethics. He seems so intent upon making us feel good, of persuading us that today is the first day of the rest of our lives, that he almost skirts the issue of our actually being good.

But psychology does not stand in opposition to ethics; it is one of its essential support systems. Repentance is a result of active personal choice. It demands a clear self-image and a strong ego structure. And Rabbi Gerondi asks us to pretend that we are born anew in order to lay out an effective course for the future. While we cannot repent an evil that we have committed if we feel no guilt, we must not be so crippled by self-recrimination that we are unable to take the ethical initiative. For God's readiness to forgive is one of Judaisms's most cherished doctrines.

The Hebrew word describing the process of repentance is "teshuvah," which means "return" - a return to the ways of God. Teshuvah, by its very nature, is directed to the future. The past is known, but the future is as yet uncharted, so we must focus on the task of spiritually strengthening ourselves. We may atone for past acts, but when we return to the ways of God, we commit ourselves to being better people in the future, so that we will be morally equipped to meet unknown challenges that will confront us.

The concept of return further teaches us that good and evil, right and wrong, are not relative ideas, subject to time, place and personal opinion. They are absolute truths, rooted in God's ways, expressed by the laws of the Torah and the interpretations of the Talmud.

Judaism argues that the individual can change and rebuild. The individual is capable of self-renewal. The individual can return to the ways of God. And most important, it is never too late to repent; God is always ready to receive us, with "His hand outstretched."

STUDY QUESTIONS

1 According to Rabbi Gerondi, repentance is a process which must be enacted or experienced by a genuinely contrite individual. Outline the steps of this process.

2 Why do the rabbis use the word "teshuvah" to describe the process of repentance? What insights can we derive from this word?

3 How does Rabbi Gerondi's understanding of man's psychological makeup encourage the individual through the process of repentance? Why is it so important for a repenting individual to cast away all feelings of guilt, and to assume the moral status of a newborn? In what sense is the memory of old sins and related guilt feelings considered an obstacle to repentance?

4 How would you explain the idea that "In the place where penitents stand, even the wholly righteous cannot stand"? Why, in your opinion, does Judaism give such precedence to the penitent?

5 Why does Rabbi Gerondi consider the future so much more important than the past? In what sense is teshuvah a commitment to the future?

6 The reading of the Book of Jonah is the focal point of the afternoon synagogue service on Yom Kippur, the Day of Atonement. This book tells the story of the prophet Jonah who, commanded by God to deliver a message of impending punishment to the pagan city of Nineveh, rebels and seeks to shun his obligation. He flees, by ship, in the opposite direction, to Tarshish. Enroute, his ship is besieged by a terrible storm which threatens the life of all on board. Jonah, understanding that the storm has been caused by his recalcitrance, offers himself as a sacrifice to be thrown overboard. The storm immediately subsides. Jonah is swallowed by a huge fish, specially prepared by God for him. In its belly he spends three days and nights, after which he prays to God and praises Him for sparing his life. The fish sends forth Jonah from its belly.

Now, when God again orders Jonah to go to Nineveh, he obeys and delivers His message to the people of the evil city. When they hear that God is angry and plans to destroy them, they repent, they mend their ways, and they seek forgiveness. God is moved by their actions, and forgives them.

This, however, does not please Jonah who would have preferred to see the evil-doers punished rather than forgiven. God makes Jonah understand His mercy by first letting a sheltering vine grow near Jonah, and then making it wither. When the man expresses his sorrow over the loss of the vine, God asks, "You cared about the plant, which you did not work for and which you did not grow, which appeared overnight and perished overnight. And should not I care about Nineveh, that great city, in which there are more than a hundred and twenty thousand persons who do not yet know their right hand from their left, and many beasts as well!"

Why do you suppose the rabbis chose the Book of Jonah to be read on Yom Kippur? What lessons does it teach?

7 One of the points made in the Book of Jonah is that not only individuals sin. At times, whole societies sin. Can you think of examples of this today? In your community? In our country? In other countries? If you were given the power to bring about one change for the better in your community, what would that change be? Why?

8 There are several prohibitions associated with the observance of Yom Kippur. They call for abstinence from eating and drinking, from washing, from using body-lotions and oils, from wearing leather shoes, and from engaging in sexual relations. Why do you think the rabbis invoked these prohibitions? How do you imagine that the abstinence from these normal, daily functions can promote individual atonement?

FOR DISCUSSION

"There is ... evidence in the Torah
that our ancestors were not untainted by
the same crimes and vices that prevailed
among other peoples. But this is true: that
the Torah and the Prophets fastened upon
the Jewish People a sense of guilt in connection with unethical conduct of all sorts.

"In our day, however, Jews have
largely lost that sense of guilt and have ac-
cepted as normal those low standards of
honesty, integrity and just dealing which
are condoned by the conventional mores of
the rest of the world. That is an alarming
situation. Unless Judaism can sensitize us
to the distinction between truth and falsehood, right and wrong, all our ado about it
is mere pretense.

"We must recover the sense of sin,
in connection with all forms of dishonesty,
all mean advantages that we take of our
neighbors to further our own interests. But,
having recovered the sense of sin, we must
not stop there ... One of the dangers we
must guard against is the inclination to
think that the pangs of remorse which we
may feel at times absolve us from the need
of genuine teshuvah or repentance, which
means a change in our whole standard of
values and pattern of behavior in our relations with our fellow men.

"Unless Judaism can give us the in-
spiration and guidance for such a change,
there is no chance of its surviving in the
Diaspora ..."

In light of your own experience as
well as what you have learned from the
teachings of Rabbi Gerondi, what is your
reaction to this quotation from the pen of
a twentieth-century rabbi, Mordecai Kap-
lan?

COMMUNITY
קהילה

SOURCE:

ETHICS OF JUDAISM

AUTHOR:

Moritz Lazarus
(1824 – 1903)

Born in Wieden, Poland, Moritz Lazarus was a professor of philosophy and the author of scholarly works in both philosophy and the psychology of nations. He believed that Jewish teachings in all areas must derive from rigorous analysis of traditional sources. He insisted that ethical values and practices were the highest form of religious expression to which even God must be held accountable.

I will be I is the formula for the state of mind in which violation of the law becomes a positive desire. Directly opposed to it is the perfect unstinting obedience of the one who makes the universal law the court of his will - who of his own accord and so far as is necessary ... lets (universal law) become the force dominating him ...

It has been shown that the Torah itself again and again emphasizes the connection existing between the notion of holiness and the notion of obedience to law.

The notion of holiness has been designated as the ethical ideal of Judaism. The sanctification of life, then, is the aim of all morality, and sanctification consists in the conception of the moral as the highest purpose in life.

Finally, it follows that sanctification of life implies the union (association) of men ... all beings called to be moral in and through reverence for law shall be bound together as a unit. For in a true and real sense, not the individual can be holy, but only the community. God is the only single being Who is holy ... throughout the Scriptures, the only ethically holy person referred to in the singular is God. Whereas holiness is mentioned in connection with other persons, it is ... applied to the whole of the people.

In what sense does "I will be I" constitute a desire to violate the law? Can't a person be self-absorbed and devoid of a commitment to the community without ever "breaking the law?"

Law is the reflection of a society's character, a translation of its values into a network of day-to-day rules, procedures and institutions. Respect for human life, for example, may be expressed through laws against murder, criminal assault and drunk driving. Respect for personal dignity may be expressed through laws against libel and arbitrary search.

What about Jewish law? The over-riding thrust of the instructions and injunctions set forth in the Torah can be summed up in a single word: community. Judaism teaches us that *"Kol Yisrael arevim zeh lazeh:* - All of Israel, the Jewish people, are responsible for one another." This is a pivotal element of our identity, expressed again and again in our history and tradition.

The laws of *Leket, Shichechah* and *Peah* are cases in point. *Leket* refers to crops that happen to fall to the ground in the course of the harvest. *Shichechah* refers to crops that the farmer has forgotten to take in during the harvest. And *Peah* refers to crops growing at the corners of the farmer's field. In each of these instances, the farmer is expressly forbidden to collect the crops in question. He is commanded to leave them so that the poor, the widowed, and the orphaned may gather them up. Our connection and commitment to one another have not been left to individual conscience; they have been written into law and constantly underscored by canon and custom.

To turn one's back on the needs of other members of the community means more than simply being ungenerous or uncaring. It means not being a good Jew. As God declares to the Jewish people through the prophet Isaiah: "Of what value to me is the multitude of your sacrifices? Your New Moons, your Sabbath ... I cannot endure injustice with solemn assemblies ... Learn to do good, seek judgment, relieve the oppressed, judge with fairness and compassion the fatherless, plead for the widow."

This belief in social justice and community involvement is Judaism's vital essence. Accordingly, people who insist that "I will be I," ignore their commitment to the community. And though they strictly obey the letter of the law, they effectively violate its ethical intention—its spirit.

Lazarus draws a further distinction between the law's letter and the law's spirit when he speaks of violation of the law as a "positive desire." This means that a person may adhere to laws of social responsibility already "on the books," but reject the values upon which these laws are based. The "I will be I" individuals may obey the law of *Leket*, for example, but turn their backs on situations of need that arise and are not specifically covered by law. When the Jews in Eastern Europe set up "eating days" for impoverished yeshivah students or contributed to dowries for poor girls, they did so, not because of the dictates of the law's letter, but because of their perception of the law's spirit.

Yet, for all his preoccupation with community, Lazarus is mindful of the needs of the individual. He speaks of "one who makes the universal law the court of his will ... of his own accord ..." That is, he conceives of the ideal community as a union of individuals who actively choose to join hands in a circle of mutual responsibility. And "so far as is necessary" is Lazarus' way of saying that a delicate balance must be struck between the demands of the community and rights of the individual. History teaches us that people in positions of authority sometimes invoke the name of the larger community as a rationalization for reducing individual freedom and expanding their own power. We must guard against that possibility by promoting the interests of the community only "so far as is necessary."

The term "universal law" points up two distinct, but closely related ideas: equality and unity. Jewish law plays no favorites; there is no selective system of justice in the Torah. All people are to be treated equally. And, as the story of the creation teaches, God is the Creator of all things. We are all ultimately united to one another. We are all members of a universal community.

What does Lazarus mean by holiness? Lazarus insists that in Judaism, holiness refers to "the notion of obedience to the law." Jewish law focuses primarily on our moral relationships with other human beings and our commitment to the community at large. And when Lazarus speaks of the sanctification of life (not merely its preservation), he means to invest it with dignity, decency, compassion and justice. It calls to mind the famous words of the sage Hillel. When challenged to sum up the meaning of the Torah while standing on one foot, Hillel replied: "What is hateful to you, do not do to your neighbor. That is the whole Torah. All the rest is commentary. Now go and study."

Finally, the statement that "God is the only single being Who is holy," underscores Judaism's profound aversion to idolatry in any form. In the Bible, no man or woman is ever called holy. The great biblical figures have been esteemed not because of a personal aura of holiness, but because of the active role they played within the community and the contribution they made to the community's growth and moral awareness.

STUDY QUESTIONS

1 How do you understand Lazarus' idea of "I will be I"? How does this approach to life express a desire to violate the law?

2 How would you explain the difference between the letter of the law and its spirit? Give an example.

3 In your own words, explain Lazarus' use of the following terms: holiness; sanctification of life; universal law.

4 Why does Judaism say that holiness does not lie in any single individual, but in the whole community? What does this mean for us in terms of our values and our way of life?

5 Narcissus was a Greek mythological character who fell in love with his own image. "Narcissism" is the term, derived from this myth, which denotes self-indulgence and self-absorption. It has been observed that narcissism is characteristic of our society; that very often, more value is given to self-contemplation and self-fulfillment than to caring for others. "Me-ism" is another term which has been used to describe a society which values self-gratification above all else. How does this attitude compare to the teachings of Judaism as expressed by Hillel "standing on one foot"? How would you explain the meaning of the story about Hillel? How would you apply these ideas to our lives today?

6 How does Lazarus express his concern for the individual? Why do you think it is so important, in Lazarus' view, for the individual to submit to universal law of his own free will? Can you point to examples, in modern times, of people in positions of authority (political leaders, religious leaders, heads of movements and causes) invoking "the good of the community" as a rationalization for reducing individual freedom and expanding their own power?

7 Can you suggest any concrete ways in which you might express your own sense of social responsibility? How can you, either as an individual or together with your friends, make your community a closer, more cohesive unit and a better place to live?

8 Today most of us live in an urban rather than agricultural setting. How might we adapt the principles of *Leket, Shichechah* and *Peah*, to life in the city or suburbs? How can we redefine and adapt the "spirit" of these laws in order to shelter the homeless, feed the poor, and generally help the disadvantaged in our modern urban society?

FOR DISCUSSION

The concept of "Kol Yisrael arevim zeh lazeh" is one of Judaism's most important values. How has this value been expressed in your community, in American Jewish life, and in the State of Israel?

SEXUALITY
מיניות

SOURCE:

IGGERET HA-KODESH (THE HOLY LETTER)

AUTHOR:

Rabbi Moses Ben-Nahman
(1194 – 1270)

Also called Nahmanides and often referred to by the initials of his name, the RaMBaN, Rabbi Moses Ben-Nahman was a physician, rabbi, philosopher, poet and author of many scholarly commentaries on the Bible and the Talmud. Nahmanides served as chief rabbi of Catalonia, Spain. He successfully represented Spanish Jewry in a public religious dispute with a convert from Judaism to Christianity and was subsequently forced to flee from Spain. He emigrated to Eretz Yisrael where he organized the remnants of the Jewish community in Jerusalem and served as a spiritual leader until his death.

now that the sexual intercourse of a man with his wife is holy and pure... No one should think that sexual intercourse is ugly and loathsome...

We the possessors of the Holy Torah believe that God... created all... and did not create anything ugly and shameful...

The mystery of man includes his being the mystery of wisdom, understanding and knowledge. Know that the male is the mystery of wisdom, and the female is the mystery of understanding. And the pure sex act is the mystery of knowledge. If so, it follows that proper sexual union can be a means of spiritual elevation when it is properly practiced, and the mystery greater than this is the secret of the heavenly bodies when they unite in the manner of man and woman.

A husband should speak with his wife with the appropriate words, some of erotic passion, some words of fear of the Lord...

A man should never force himself upon his wife and never overpower her, for the Divine Spirit never rests upon one whose conjugal relations occur in the absence of desire, love and free will...

One should never argue with his wife, and certainly never strike her on account of sexual matters. The Talmud... tells us that just as a lion tears at his prey and eats it shamelessly, so does an ignorant man shamelessly strike and sleep with his wife...

A man should not have intercourse with his wife while she is asleep, for then they cannot both agree to the act. It is far better to arouse her with words that will placate her and inspire desire in her.

To conclude, when you are ready for sexual union, see that your wife's intentions combine with yours. Do not hurry to arouse her until she is receptive. Be calm, as you enter the path of love and will.

Sex, love and marriage have been frequent topics of discussion in Jewish thinking. In the second chapter of The Book of Genesis, it is written: "Hence a man leaves his father and mother, and clings to his wife so that they become one flesh."

In the SONG OF SONGS, we read:
"How sweet is your love
My own, my bride!
How much more delightful
your love than wine."

The Talmud teaches us: "A man who does not have a wife lives without joy, without blessings, and without goodness..." And the Zohar declares: "When there is no union of male and female, men are not worthy of beholding the Shekhinah (the Divine Presence)..." There have been Jewish thinkers who refer to sexuality as the "Evil Impulse," with the power to corrupt our character and divert us from the path of righteousness, but this poses no real contradiction. Rather, the sex drive is perceived as a dynamic force which can be used either to create and enhance, or to degrade and destroy. What sex is *not* considered, however, is unnatural, or in any way removed from a healthy, wholesome existence. All of our leaders have had wives. And celibacy has never been heralded as a holy state of being, or in any sense, spiritually admirable.

Nahmanides' writings attest that we have not been free of ambivalence and confusion in the sphere of human sexuality. People were as concerned about sexual relations in Nahmanides' time as they are today. In the final analysis, as Nahmanides illustrates, sexual issues are human issues, and the overriding concerns are not about matters of procedure or technique, but rather about ethics. Where do our sexual needs fit into the religious and moral scheme of things? In what manner does "having sex" grow into the process of "making love?" How do we relate to one another, and what are our emotional responsibilities to one another? Nahmanides addresses two fundamental questions. First, what is the Jewish view of sexual relations? And second, how must we conduct ourselves in its performance?

Nahmanides places human sexuality in the mainstream of religious definition and moral responsibility. Sexual intercourse, he insists, is "holy and pure," because it is created by God. It is an expression of God's will. Jews constantly try to translate God's will into a way of life. Accordingly, our sexual relations, no less than any other aspect of our day-to-day existence, must reflect and be accountable to Judaism's values.

The use of the word "mystery" offers an important insight into Judaism's vision of sexuality. Nahmanides speaks of mystery in its unlimited sense, as an ever-unfolding dimension of human possibility. And while he draws a line of distinction between the respective mysteries of the male and female, he never suggests that one is in any way superior to the other. Indeed, the essential equality between the sexes is underscored by the third mystery, the mystery of knowledge - the sex act itself.

The connection between sexuality and knowledge is not Nahmanides' invention. In the Bible, the word used to describe the act of sexual intercourse is "to know." This signifies intimate communication. And communication, in its truest sense, grows out of a relationship between equals.

Equality serves as the basis of Judaism's key sexual values. When Nahmanides declares that "a man should speak to his wife..." he invests the principle of pleasure with sensitivity and consideration. "A man should never force himself..." underscores the idea that marriage is not a license to self-indulgence, but a framework for participants to awaken their desire and nourish their love. "One should never argue..." takes aim at sexual aggression, asserting that we deserve to be treated gently and with dignity. And the fact that "a man should not have intercourse with his wife while she is asleep..." teaches that gentleness is in itself not sufficient. The freedom of will and action must be fully acknowledged and respected. This is the ultimate meaning of love. Finally, the references to God and the Torah and Talmud remind us that sexual relations are a part of - never apart from - Judaism's way of life.

STUDY QUESTIONS

1 Which arguments does Nahmanides present to support his position that sexual intercourse is not "ugly and loathsome"?

2 Nahmanides seems to be reacting to sexual abuses which existed in his society. What do you think these abuses were?

3 What do you consider the main sexual problem in our society? Can you point to the causes of this problem?

4 Most people agree that we have undergone a sexual revolution in recent years. What do you think are its key issues?

5 In what sense does Nahmanides use the term "mystery"? How, specifically, would you explain the "mystery" of wisdom and the "mystery" of understanding? Do you agree with the distinction he draws between the respective natures of men and women? What does he mean by the "mystery" of knowledge, and what does this term reveal about the Jewish view of sexual intercourse?

6 Imagine that a non-Jewish friend asks you about Judaism's approach to sex, love, and marriage. On the basis of Nahmanides' essay and the traditional sources quoted in the chapter, how would you characterize this point of view?

7 How would you explain the concept of "love and will" as it is set forth by Nahmanides?

8 What are the specific values pertaining to sexual relations which can be drawn from Nachmanides' essay? Can they pertain to a sexual relationship in which the parties are not married?

FOR DISCUSSION

Two pervasive attitudes which tend to diminish respect for women are sexual harassment on the job and the response to rape wherein the victim bears the responsibility. The statements that, "She must have been asking for it!"; "With what she was wearing what do you expect?"; "Boys will be boys!" characterize these attitudes. What is your response to these remarks? How would you go about countering the attitudes they betray?

SUCCESS
הצלחה

SOURCE:

HOVOT HA-LEVAVOT
(DUTIES OF THE HEART)

AUTHOR:

Bahya Ben Joseph Ibn Paquda
(Second half of 11th Century)

A poet and philosopher, Bahya Ben Joseph Ibn Paquda produced the first major work in classical ethical Jewish literature. His Duties of the Heart, *published at the end of the eleventh century, was widely regarded as the most influential body of thought in this sphere for over six hundred years. Ibn Paquda set forth ten fundamental moral principles, each constituting a separate chapter, and each based upon a religious attitude. His concern was with the inner quality of Jewish life, as distinguished from such outward actions as ritual, prayer, and study.*

A person should take account with his soul when he impetuously and industriously applies himself to his worldly interests, which he seeks to further with the utmost energy and keenest planning to the limit of his power . . .

He will then find that his thought on worldly affairs is the highest of his thoughts, and his hopes thereon are the loftiest of his expectations, so that none of his various kinds of possessions is sufficient for him. He is like fire, which blows more fiercely the more wood is added to it. So, too, his heart and intent draw him day and night to his worldly interest . . .

He looks forward to seasons when merchandise should be accumulated and to the seasons when it should be sold. He studies market conditions, investigates cheapness or dearness of goods, and notes whether prices are falling in all parts of the world. Neither heat nor cold, neither storm on the sea, nor length of journeys in the desert deters him from traveling to distant places.

He does all this in the hope of reaching an end in a matter wherein there is no end and where there is a possibility that his exertions will be in vain, yielding nothing but protracted pain, trouble, and labor. And if he attains a little of what he hopes for, possibly all that he will have of it will be the taking of it, managing it, and carefully saving it from mishaps, until it comes into the possession of the one for whom it was decreed.

Most people want to achieve success in their business and professional lives, and are willing to work hard to realize this aim. And yet, success is frequently depicted in questionable or even negative terms. This is not to say that success is an evil, but rather that the road to "making it" may be marked by moral pitfalls and human contradictions.

Bahya Ben Joseph Ibn Paquda was keenly aware of the conflict of values inherent in the pursuit of money and status. He challenged us to impart to our lives something more precious and lasting than the relentless making of money and gathering of goods.

We learn from Ibn Paquda's essay that "making it" was as absorbing an aim nearly a thousand years ago as it is today. He sets forth, in grim graphic detail, the spiritual and intellectual emptiness that can be the consequence of our quest for more and more. Thus, "...his thoughts on worldly affairs is the highest of all of his thoughts, and his hopes therein are the loftiest of his expectations..." And he characterizes this preoccupation in terms not so much of ambition, but of mindless addiction. So, "...none of his various kinds of possessions is sufficient for him ... So, too, his heart and intent draw him day and night to his worldly interest..." Finally, he warns us of the futility of so singleminded a focus: "...He does all this in the hope of reaching an end in the matter where there is no end and where there is a possibility that his exertions will be in vain..."

What, then, would Ibn Paquda have us do? He does not urge us to turn our backs on material rewards. Rather, he counsels each of us "to take account with his soul..." Taking account implies a process of looking inward to define our needs, examine our values, and create our priorities accordingly.

This ethic finds frequent expression in our history, our tradition, and our culture. Our patriarchs were men of means. But their most heralded qualities lay in their special relationships with God and their roles as the originators of the Jewish nation. The laws of the Torah and the teachings of the prophets dwell not upon the glories of achieving success, but upon the values of human compassion and social responsibility. The overwhelming majority of our heroes have been scholars, teachers and thinkers. In the world of our Eastern European great-grandparents, the highest status was accorded to those who excelled in the study of Torah and Talmud. Of course, individuals of great wealth have won acclaim in the annals of our people, but their place in history has rested not upon the accumulation of wealth as such, but upon service to the community.

In sum, Ibn Paquda says that making a good living is important. But let us not get so involved in its details that we lose sight of a far more essential goal—that of making a life.

STUDY QUESTIONS

1 "Success" is not an immutable value. It has different meanings for different people, and even different meanings to people at different stages of their lives. At this point in your life, how do you perceive "success"? What has influenced you most in these feelings?

2 Why do you think that people are willing to work so hard and to give up so much in order to achieve "success"? Why is the pursuit of success so often characterized in negative terms?

3 One might say to Ibn Paquda: "You make some interesting points, but you have no idea of the pressures I'm up against. Everyone, and everything in my cultural environment steers me toward "success". There is a stiff social and psychological price to pay for not being successful!" Do you agree with this statement? Does it apply to you? What is the nature of the price you would pay for non-success (or failure)? Where does the pressure to succeed come from, and what form does it take?

4 It has been pointed out that our lives can be compared to a balancing act, juggling various needs and demands. As we grow older, the choices become more complicated. Can you think of examples of difficult or painful choices that you have had to make in your own life? What values were involved in the making of these choices?

5 What do you learn from Ibn Paquda about the pitfalls of overriding ambition? What inferences can we make as we set our own priorities?

6 Success has been characterized as a "pot of gold at the end of the rainbow", "hitting the jackpot", and even "reaching the moon". What do these images tell us about the nature of success? One writer coined the phrase "bitch-goddess success". How do you understand this phrase? Can you cite examples of success being held up as an object of worship? What price is often extorted by this goddess for her "blessing" of success?

7 Ibn Paquda characterizes the pursuit of money and success not so much in terms of ambition as of addiction. Why do we become so hooked? Why is there so often no such thing as "enough"? Can you point to forces within our own society and culture that encourage and reinforce this chronic dissatisfaction? What materialistic forces are represented by the following terms: status symbol, consumer culture, built-in obsolescence, keeping up with the Joneses?

8 Ibn Paquda teaches that the single-minded pursuit of money and success is more often than not an exercise in emptiness and futility. How does he support this belief?

FOR DISCUSSION

Ibn Paquda tells us that there is a lot more to life than merely making money or achieving success. What are the specific ingredients of "a lot more"? What is your idea of a rich, full life? Imagine that you've just won ten million dollars in your state's lottery. What would you do with your newly found wealth? How would you live your life?

BUSINESS

עסקים

SOURCE:
SEFER HASIDIM (BOOK OF THE PIOUS)

AUTHOR:
Judah Ben-Samuel He-Hasid
(c. 1150 – 1217)

One of the key figures in the Hasidei Ashkenaz movement, Judah Ben-Samuel He-Hasid was a prominent theologian and ethical thinker. Yet, very little is known about him, in part due to his extreme humility. He refused to put his name to his works, which led to a great deal of scholarly speculation as to what he did and did not write, and to the creation of many popular legends about him. Judah Ben-Samuel He-Hasid is believed to be the main author of Sefer Hasidim *(The Book of the Pious).*

Never shrink (in a business dealing) from declaring that you are a Jew.

Do not purposely mislead anyone, Jew or non-Jew. In your business dealings, do not say that a certain price has been offered for your merchandise if that is not true.

Do no injustice to anyone, not even those of a different faith.

Call the attention of a non-Jew to an error that he has made in overpaying you, for it is better that you live on charity than that you disgrace the Jewish name by cheating.

Ethical business practices have always been one of Judaism's urgent moral concerns. The Torah, the Talmud, and a host of later writings grapple with every manner of issue related to business ethics. In the Bible, the book of Leviticus instructs us not to "falsify measure of length, weight or capacity." The book of Deuteronomy warns that any businessman "who deals dishonestly is abhorrent to the Lord your God." The prophet Amos lashes out at those "who devour the needy, annihilating the poor of the land, saying: 'If only the New Moon were over, so that we could sell grain, the Sabbath, so that we could offer wheat for sale... tilting a dishonest scale and selling grain refuse as grain.'"

At first glance, the excerpts from Sefer Hasidim sound more like public relations than business ethics. And surely, because of our longstanding status as a minority group, there has been a need to put on our "best face" for the outside world. On one level there is a public relations factor implied, but the premise upon which it rests is not image-projection, but unity - the unity of the Jewish people. As Jews, we are linked to one another. The problems of one Jewish community are the problems of all Jewish communities. Unity is a pivotal component of our Jewishness; how a Jew behaves in business concerns all Jews. And so, Rabbi Judah teaches us that "...it is better that you live on charity than that you disgrace the Jewish name by cheating..."

If Rabbi Judah is concerned about disgracing the Jewish name, why does he instruct those who are engaged in business to "never shrink from declaring that you are a Jew?" The key to understanding once again lies in a concept of unity - the unity that must bind Jewish identity to Jewish ideals. In the absence of this unity, moral fragmentation takes place. It is this fragmentation that is at the root of the prophet Amos' rage at those who observe the Sabbath and at the same time hatch schemes to devour the needy. The Lord, declares Amos, "will never forget any of their doings," will never tolerate the convenient dividing line that some draw between expressions of identity (holiday observance) and the practice of ideals (fair business dealings).

Money is the overriding symbol of the "real" world, wherein the principles we profess are put to the test of practical application. A truly pious Jew cannot be dishonest in business; this would be a contradiction in terms. And when we declare that we are Jews, as Rabbi Judah would have us do, we are saying, "This is what we believe and this is what we will practice in the arena of business transactions."

Finally, when Rabbi Judah instructs "Do no injustice to those of different faith," he carries the concept of unity and his injunction against fragmentation to its logical culmination - the universal sphere. Business ethics must not stop at the boundaries of Jewish communal life. We must not practice selective morality. We must behave as Jews at all times, and with all people.

STUDY QUESTIONS

1 The imperative to provide honest weights and measures mentioned in the Bible is emphasized by the rabbis. Their teachings encompass all transactions, from the most elaborate and costly to the most mundane and minor. They teach us to be concerned with the weight of cheese and beans as much as with the weight of diamonds and gold. What is the greater moral implication of an ounce of cheese, more or less, on the scale of a Jewish storekeeper?

2 The noted 18th century ethical writer, Rabbi Zevi Hirsch Koidonover remarked, "True piety is determined by one's attitude toward money, for only he who is reliable in money matters may be considered pious..." What is your reaction to this statement? Is it valid?

3 Is it true, in your opinion, that what one Jew does reflects upon and affects all Jews? Explain your feelings.

4 Why does Rabbi Judah the Pious insist that in any business that we transact, we must never shrink from declaring that we are Jews?

5 The Jews have been called the "Chosen People". How does the mantle of chosen-ness affect the ethical responsibility the Jew bears toward other Jews, and toward the world at large? If an individual's actions might bring shame on the Jewish community, why are we not taught to hide our identity in the world at large?

6 From what we have read in this chapter, how do you think Rabbi Judah would respond to the following statements:

"Let the buyer beware."

"My goods are for sale here as you see them, and this is their price. It's up to you to decide whether you want them or not."

"I'm no angel in business. But I'm a good Jew. I would never cheat one of my own."

7 In this chapter, what are the three ways in which the author conceives of "unity" as it pertains to the Jewish people?

8 On the basis of what you have read in this chapter, how would you complete the following sentence: "A good Jew is one who..."

9 Your kid brother feels enterprising and decides to open a lemonade stand in front of your house on a hot day.

By the end of the afternoon, he faces the dilemma of a growing demand and a dwindling supply. (All the neighborhood stores have closed for the day.) As he reaches the end of his stock of fresh lemons he has to decide whether to dilute his original recipe with a greater percentage of water, pour less than a full cup for each new customer, or just close up shop when the original supply runs out. What advice and ethical guidelines might you give him?

FOR DISCUSSION

One of the most successful and visible aspects of modern business is the advertising industry. It deals in glamor and fantasy in its efforts to make its subjects desirable. Sometimes advertisers go beyond the bounds of total truth and honesty in order to sell their goods. Although advertising is, in this country, regulated to some extent by law, the methods used by the industry often fall short of the high ethical standards we have discussed in this chapter.

Bring in three ads from a recent newspaper or magazine. Analyze them according to the following:

What is the main message of the ad?

To whom is it addressed?

What are the primary images utilized?

Is there anything illogical, inconsistent or misrepresentative in the message?

How would you advertise this product following the ethical principles set forth in this chapter?

TZEDAKAH
צדקה

SOURCES:

FOLKTALES

AUTHORS:

Unknown

Jewish folklore contains a vast body of ethical literature. There are fables, legends, stories, and wise sayings, designed not only to entertain, but to teach, as well. The overriding purpose of Jewish ethical writing is to reach as many people as possible, including members of the community with little or no education. Folk culture thus served as a singularly effective medium of communication.

A certain pious man had inherited great wealth. On the Sabbath eve, he would begin preparing for the Sabbath-hours before sundown.

One time he had to leave his home shortly before the Sabbath because of urgent business. On the way back, a poor man begged him for money to help buy provisions for the Sabbath.

The pious man angrily scolded the poor man, "How could you have waited until the last minute to buy your Sabbath fare? Nobody waits so long. You must be trying to trick me into giving you money!"

When he came home, he told his wife the story of the poor man he had met.

"I must tell you that you are wrong," his wife answered. "In your whole life you have never tasted poverty and have no idea what it is like to be poor ... I grew up in a poor home. I remember many times when it was almost dark and time for the Sabbath, and my father would still be looking for even a piece of dry bread to bring home to his family. You have sinned toward that poor man!"

When the pious man heard this, he ran about the neighborhood to find the pauper, who was still seeking Sabbath food. The rich man gave the poor man bread and fish and meat and wine for the Sabbath. Then he begged his forgiveness.

A certain man had been selfish all his life. When he was dying, his family urged him to eat. "If you give me a boiled egg," he said, "I will eat it."

As he was about to eat, a poor man appeared at his doorstep and begged, "Give me charity!" The dying man turned to his family and ordered them to give the beggar his egg.

Three days later the man died. Some time afterward, the dead man appeared to his son, who asked him, "Father, what is it like in the world to which you have gone?"

His father answered, "Make it your practice to perform charity, and you will gain a place in the world to come. Throughout my life the only act of charity that I ever performed was giving that egg to the poor man. Yet, when I died, the egg outweighed all the sins I had committed, and I was admitted to Paradise."

Of him it is said: Never refrain from doing good!

Our current reaction to the condition of poverty is often marked by bureaucractic impersonality. We tend to regard the destitute and the displaced as inhabitants of a world apart from our own. We relate to the poor in the abstract, not as fellow citizens in trouble or as neighbors in need.

The plight of the poor has always been at the center of Jewish consciousness. In the Book of Deuteronomy we read: "If there is a needy person among you... give to him readily... and the Lord your God will bless you... For there will never cease to be needy ones in your land. Which is why I command you to open your hand to the poor and needy kinsman in your land."

The words "needy kinsman in your land" underscore the idea that we are all members of the same community. The bonds that bind us together are far stronger than the circumstances that may separate us. And since "there will never cease to be needy ones in your land," our responsibility to the poor cannot be expressed as a random spurt of generosity; it must be incorporated into our way of life as an ongoing value and tradition.

These elements are woven into the first folktale. Both the rich man and the poor man are engaged in the same activity - honoring the Sabbath. They are equals in the eyes of God, united in the fulfillment of Sabbath observance. It was not enough for the rich man to finally give his less fortunate neighbor Sabbath provisions; he also begged his forgiveness for having demeaned his dignity with harsh words.

The person who called the rich man's attention to what he had done was his wife. She had herself grown up in a poor home. Poverty is never far removed from our experience. None of us can ignore its presence. As the Talmud teaches: "There is an ever-rotating wheel in this world. He who is rich today may not be so tomorrow." Possessions are impermanent. We cannot be defined by what we have, only by what we do. The only lasting reality is our way of life and the good deeds we perform.

This is precisely the point of the second folktale. God places such a premium upon the act of helping the poor, that it can cancel out a lifetime of selfishness. God is always ready to receive the penitent, and there is no better way to express "teshuvah" (returning to the ways of God) than by the performance of a good deed.

In our tradition, every holiday and festive occasion is enhanced by the mitzvah of giving to the poor. And it is not only the giving that is important, but the manner of giving as well. At the beginning of the Passover Seder, for example, we recite: "Let all those who are hungry enter and eat..." The poor and hungry are not only to be fed; they are to be invited to sit at our table. Every person is equal before God.

The personal dignity of those who receive charity must be protected. This concern underlies the eight degrees of charity set forth by Maimonides:

The highest degree... the person who provides a loan, offers a business partnership or helps find employment...

A step below... the person who gives alms so that the giver does not know to whom he gives and the recipient does not know from whom he takes...

The next rank... the person who drops money into the charity box.

A step lower... the poor person knows from whom he is taking, but the giver does not know to whom he is giving.

The next degree lower... the person who, with his own hand, bestows a gift before the poor person asks.

The next degree lower... the person who gives only after the poor person asks.

The next degree lower... the person who gives less than is fitting but gives with a gracious mien.

The lowest degree... the person who gives morosely.

The Hebrew word for charity is tzedakah which also means justice and righteousness. The act of giving morally enhances the giver as much as it materially helps the receiver. Thus the Talmud says: "Even a poor man who lives off charity should perform acts of charity."

STUDY QUESTIONS

1 The Jewish tradition asserts that "There will never cease to be needy ones in your land." (Deut. 15:11) Demonstrate the validity of this statement from your own observations.

2 In the first folktale, why did the rich man feel obliged to apologize to the poor man? Why is it important to the story that it was his wife who called the rich man's attention to the wrong he had committed?

3 In the second folktale, what is the significance of the man's being on his deathbed? An egg symbolizes life and all its potential. What bearing does this symbolism have on this tale?

4 Not everyone believes that the poor are worthy of being helped. They contend that each person is responsible for his or her own self, and that the poor are disadvantaged only because of their own laziness. What is the Jewish view of the worthiness of helping the poor?

5 Why is extending our hands to help the poor one of the key elements in our celebration of Jewish holidays and festivals?

6 Maimonides' writings have as much meaning for us today as they did for his contemporaries. The following statements are twentieth century expressions of eight attitudes of giving. Rank them in relation to Maimonides' eight degrees of charity.

Mr. A. "Here, take this. I'd like to give more but things have been a little tight for me this past week."

Ms. B. "I'm really moved by the conditions of these people and I want to help. I'm going to give you this sum of money. I know that you will distribute it with wisdom and compassion. I don't need to know any more about it."

Mr. C. "You must need some bread for your wife and children, if not for yourself. So please, not another word, no false pride. Take my check and use it well."

Ms. D. "I know you're having a hard time. Who of us isn't? Here, take this, and then get off my back! I have enough troubles of my own!"

Mr. E. "Here's my idea. Let's you and I and all the other businessmen in this neighborhood set up a revolving fund to provide low-interest loans for poor people who want to start their own businesses. And sure, more is involved than just money; part of the revolving fund will be our knowledge and our experience. Basically, we'll be helping them to help themselves."

Ms. F. "Of course I'll help out. Why didn't you let me know that you needed money? You know that all you had to do was ask."

Mr. G. "I don't know who needs what- or how much. I'm leaving a sum of money on the table. Let those who really and truly need it, divide it up among themselves. No questions asked!"

Ms. H. "I make regular yearly contributions to worthy causes, both here and abroad. And I intend to keep on doing it."

7 What is the significance of the triple meaning of the word "tzedakah"? Why must a person who lives off charity perform acts of charity in his or her right?

FOR DISCUSSION

Perhaps poverty will, indeed, always be with us. We can, however, make significant contributions toward combatting its evil effects.

Have the members of the class assume the roles of members of the City Council. The task of this group is to come up with a "game plan" to wage a war against poverty- a plan that would be practical and capable of producing long-term benefits. How would you go about doing it? What would be the main elements of such a plan? What would be the major obstacles that you are likely to encounter, and how would you deal with them? From what you know of your community, in which areas of need are you likely to make the most progress? The least progress?

STUDY
לימוד

SOURCE:

THE SILVER BOWL (KA' ARAT KESEF)

AUTHOR:

Jehoseph Ezobi
(13th Century)

Born in France, Jehoseph Ezobi came from a well-known, highly educated family. He wrote this poem, translated from the Hebrew, for his son on the occasion of his wedding. It enjoyed widespread popularity among European Jews for centuries afterward. The poem takes its title from its 130 verses which correspond to the weight of the silver bowl (130 shekels) offered by each of the princes of the twelve biblical tribes at the dedication of the priestly altar.

THE SILVER BOWL

My darling son, thou art my soul's delight,
My hope, my joy, my strength in thee unite!
Peace to thee, peace, my glory and my love,
Thy will is God's, its fruit is Heaven above.
The song I sing is thine, accept the gift,
'Tis offered to thy soul, with heart uplift . . .
My son, a 'Silver Bowl' of poesy,
Thy father's gift, thy father Ezobi . . .
The Silver Bowl is filled with songs of Truth:
Rejoice! but turn it not upon its mouth.
List now, my son, accept this gift divine,
A father's gift, whose soul, whose life is thine.
A wedding gift, to smooth thy path most fit,
Above all festive song, all clam'rous wit . . .
Its weight is measured as the priestly bowl,
When brought to God, to cleanse the erring soul.
From thee with this reward I am content,
An honoured name, a life in virtue spent.

Seek men of virtue, goodness, knowledge, truth,
Honour their crown of years, waste not thy youth...
Seek not youth's counsel, it is worse than guilt.
Its castle totters, as on ruins built.
To teachers, not to books entrust thy mind;
Thy soul to living words, not dead, e'er bind...
Put not thy faith in Grecian sophistry:
To climb its vineyard's fence no man is free.
Its draught will make thy footsteps vacillate
From truth; will make thy heart to curse and hate.
But askest thou in what to seek thy lore,
In grammar much, but in the Talmud more....
And when the day of good report is nigh
E'en as Elijah thou shalt rise on high.
Three crowns there are, and these the world may love;
A blameless name is more, all crowns above.

One of the most joyous events in Jewish life, the wedding ceremony, appears at first glance to be a ritual of separation. Marriage signifies a cutting loose from family of origin, and the creation of a new family nucleus. Yet this ritual is, in fact, not an act of breaking away, but a commitment to continuity. It can be viewed as an expression not of "freedom from" previous ties and obligations, but of "freedom to" embrace these ties and obligations as a matter of active personal choice. Marriage can mean setting up a framework of family and home within which Judaism's traditions may find expression and flourish. Thus, continuity is not an exercise in nostalgia, but an act of renewal, a dynamic coming together of past, present and future. And how do we achieve this aim? Through a process of study - study of the Torah, the Talmud, and other traditional sources - a process of study that begins when we are old enough to read, and continues throughout our lives.

It was in this spirit that Ezobi sent his son a poem as a wedding gift. The poem suggests a deeply rooted structure of intellectual and moral authority that encompassed both father and son, transcending the boundaries of conventional family ties. Both father and son studied Judaism's precepts and strictures. They thought about them, interpreted them, and applied them to situations that arose in their daily lives. It was this activity that effectively bridged the distance of years, physical separation, and differing concerns.

Even when Ezobi warns of the dangers of assimilation, he focuses on its intellectual aspect. He speaks in terms of attitude, approach and a way of thinking and looking at the world. "Put not thy faith in Greek sophistry," he instructs his son, "...seek thy lore in grammar much, but in Talmud more."

Why does Ezobi place such emphasis on grammar? Because he wishes to discuss not only what to study, but how to study. It is here that he illuminates the ethical dimension of this activity. Ethics is a product of free will. It involves a definition of self, relationships with others, and responsibilities to the community at large. Such a process demands rigorous thought and disciplined expression; these are the underpinnings of logic and understanding.

We are commanded to study our tradition, not merely to memorize it or to keep it around for ready reference. We are commanded to read it again and again, to think about it and discuss it, to mull over its meaning, to constantly formulate fresh insights and interpretations, and to translate its teachings into the idiom of our immediate experience. And so it is "...to teacher, not to books entrust thy mind. Thy soul to living words..." We are the People of the Book, but the Book is to be learned, not worshipped. The Torah is no idol to be enshrined in marble, but a legacy of living words that responds to the challenges of changing times.

In sum, Jewish continuity is nurtured by study. Not an uncritical veneration of the past, but an honest, energetic dialogue between "then" and "now" and "what will come to pass."

STUDY QUESTIONS

1 Newlyweds receive beautiful objects for their home. Silver items are often among them. In this poem a real bowl is not the gift. Rather, the poem itself is. Why do you think Ezobi chose the image of a silver bowl for his poetic gift?

2 What do you think Ezobi means when he says, "Seek not youth's counsel... Its castle totters..."

Do you agree with this idea? Did you ever turn to an older person for advice with a personal problem? How was their advice different from what your peers might have told you?

3 People can learn from books and from teachers. Ezobi says, "To teachers, not to books entrust thy mind..." If you had a choice to learn only from books or only from teachers which would you choose? Why?

4 The Sophists to whom the author refers were Greek philosophers who valued rhetoric over true knowledge. In other words, they cared more about how they said something than what it was they said. Medieval grammarians, on the other hand, sought to know and understand the world through the study of the structure of language. Why do you think the poet says, "Put not thy faith in Grecian sophistry... But askest thou in what to seek thy lore, In grammar much, but in the Talmud more..."

5 According to Jewish tradition, it is Elijah the Prophet who is to herald the coming of the Messiah (or the Messianic Era). Why does the author refer to Elijah in this poem?

6 The poet claims that a "blameless name" is the most coveted reward. In other words, a good reputation is the most valuable asset we can have. How do you see the relationship between study, knowledge and a good name?

7 Ezobi wrote his poem in the twelfth century, eight hundred years ago. His world was very different from ours. What meaning can his values of learning and study have for us in our modern age of computers, space travel and nuclear capabilities? If he were alive today, what do you think his thoughts would have been concerning the Challenger tragedy?

FOR DISCUSSION

Ezobi admonishes his son to entrust his mind to teachers rather than to books. What is the danger in this advice? Under what circumstances might a teacher tell you not to read certain books, or forbid you to discuss certain ideas or events? Should a teacher have this power? In what ways can censorship be good? In what ways, not good?

DERECH ERETZ
דרך ארץ

SOURCE:

ETHICAL WILL

AUTHOR:

Eleazar of Mayence
(12th Century)

Respected as a singularly pious man, the humility of Eleazar of Mayence is attested to by the title of his ethical will, "The Ideals of an Average Jew." In it, he sets forth the principles and practices of living a good Jewish life. Written in Germany in the 12th century, Eleazar's will was later published by his grandson and namesake. A Jewish ethical will is a testament composed by a parent as a legacy for his children. The underlying assumption of an ethical will is that an individual's most cherished possessions are not material goods, but a way of life (Derech Eretz).

These are the things which my sons and daughters shall do at my request. They shall go to the house of prayer morning and evening... they shall occupy themselves with the Torah, the Psalms, or with works of charity. Their business must be conducted honestly, in their dealings both with Jew and Gentile. They must be gentle in their manner, and prompt to accede to every honorable request. They must not talk more than is necessary, by this will they be saved from slander, falsehood, and frivolity. They shall give (charity) an exact tithe (ten percent) of all their possessions; they shall never turn away a poor man empty-handed, but must give him what they can, be it much or little...

My daughters must obey scrupulously the rules applying to women: modesty, sanctity, reverence should mark their married lives...

they must respect their husbands and must be invariably amiable to them. Husbands, on their part, must honor their wives more than themselves, and treat them with tender consideration.

If they can by any means contrive it, my sons and daughters should live in communities, and not isolated from other Jews, so that their sons and daughters may learn the ways of Judaism. Even if compelled to solicit from others the money to pay a teacher, they must not let the young, of both sexes, go without instruction in the Torah...

I earnestly beg my children to be tolerant and humble to all... Should cause for dissension present itself be slow to accept the quarrel... Even if you suffer loss thereby, forbear and forgive, for God has many ways of feeding and sustaining His creatures. To the slanderer do not retaliate... though it be proper to rebut false accusation, yet it is most desirable to set an example of reticence... You yourselves must avoid uttering any slander... In trade be true, never grasping at what belongs to another. For by avoiding these wrongs - slander, falsehood, money-grubbing - men will surely find tranquillity and affection...

Be on your guard concerning vows, and cautious as to promises... speak always of the 'Creator, blessed be He,' and in all that you propose to do, today or tomorrow, add the proviso, 'if the Lord wills, I shall do this thing.' Thus remember God's part in your life...

Whatever happiness befalls you, be it in monetary fortunes, or in the birth of children, or any other of the many blessings which may come to you, be not stolidly unappreciative, like dumb cattle that utter no word of gratitude. But offer praises to the Rock (God) who has befriended you... When words of gratitude are used in the liturgy, pause to reflect in silence on the goodness of God to you that day...

Every one of these good qualities becomes habitual with him who studies the Torah: for that study leads to the formation of noble character...

And my sons and daughters, keep yourselves far from the snare of frivolous conversation, which begins in tribulation and ends in destruction. Nor be you found in the company of these light talkers. Judge... every man charitably and use your best efforts to detect an honorable explanation of conduct, however suspicious. Try to persuade yourselves that it was your neighbor's zeal for some good end that led him to the conduct you deplore.

On holidays and festivals and Sabbaths seek to make happy the poor, the unfortunate, widows and orphans, who should always be guests at your tables; their joyous entertainment is a religious duty.

And as you speak no scandal, so listen to none, for if there were no receiver there would be no bearers of slanderous tales.

Be of the first ten in Synagogue... Pray steadily with the congregation, giving due value to every letter and word... if you can perform an act of loving kindness, it is accounted as equal to the study of the Law...

The Jewish ethical will was, among other things, an effort to bridge the gap between generations, to reach out and transcend the barriers of time and experience. This testament was composed by the parent, usually the father, as a legacy of religious and moral instruction for his children.

The underlying assumptions of the ethical will were that an individual's most cherished possessions are not material goods, but a way of life informed by study, prayer, strong family relationships, a commitment to the Jewish community and the Jewish people, compassion and good deeds. There can be a flow of continuity between the successive generations - a common language of shared traditions and beliefs.

Although the earliest written ethical will on record appeared in the middle of the eleventh century, the tradition of transmitting moral teachings to the next generation dates back to the days of the biblical patriarchs. Thus God says of Abraham: "I have known him (Abraham) to the end that he may command his children and his household after him, that they may keep the way of the Lord (Genesis 18:19).

And the Midrash tells us that when ... "Jacob felt that his end was near, and sought the divine mercy, 'Ruler of the World,' he cried, 'Take not my soul until I have exhorted my children!' And his wish was granted." Variations of these inter-generational instructions can be found in the stories of Moses, the Kings and the Later Prophets, as well as in legends and wisdom literature.

Judaism is often described as having created a community rooted in time, as well as space. The holy Covenant forged between God and Abraham, and later with Moses, encompasses all the generations that will come into being in the future. The Passover Seder is, at core, an act of telling the story of freedom and translating its lessons into the idiom of each succeeding generation's ideas and experiences. The Talmud applies the laws of the Torah to new situations. And when the prophet Malachi talks about the Lord's Day that will come to pass in a peaceful blessed future, he proclaims: "And God shall turn the heart of the fathers to the children, and the heart of the children to their fathers."

STUDY QUESTIONS

1 Translated literally, Derech Eretz means "way of the land" or "way of the world", the implication being "a way of life". Translated more broadly, this Hebrew term encompasses the totality of the ideal conduct of a proper Jewish life. In the ethical sense, the term Derech Eretz expresses an attitude of respect for all people in their relationships to each other, to the material world about them, and to God. Why do you think this term was chosen to be the chapter heading for the discussion of an ethical will?

2 Derech Eretz is an umbrella term under which all Jewish ethics are gathered. In this book we have dealt with these ethical topics: Free Will, Community, Sexuality, Helping the Poor, Responsible Speech, Study, Business, Success, and Repentance. Eleazar, in his will, addresses his children in regard to these same ethical topics. Choose any six sentences from Eleazar's will, and relate each to one of the chapter topics of this book.

3 While you were answering Question 2, you may have noticed that some ideas expressed in Eleazar's will could be categorized under more than one ethical heading. For example, the sentence, "For by avoiding these wrongs - slander, falsehood, moneygrubbing - men will surely find tranquillity and affection ..." could have been included in the chapter on responsible speech, business, or success. Find at least one more example from Eleazar's will, to illustrate this interrelationship of ethical concepts.

4 Keeping in mind the discussion about the comprehensive nature of the term Derech Eretz, as well as the results of the analytical exercise in Question 3, we begin to comprehend the basic unity of the Jewish ethical outlook. All of its subjects are related and interrelated. It is an integrated ethic in which conceptualized attitudes embody its values, while its conceptualized values embody all of its attitudes. Dealing with just the topics included in this volume, we see the broader subjects of Community and Free Will as larger all-inclusive values, and the more discrete topics of Sexuality, Helping the Poor, Success, Responsible Speech, Study, Business and Repentance as the particular attitudes of these values.

 A. Review the chapters on Free Will, Study and Repentance. What is their relationship?

 B. Review the chapters on Community, Business, and Helping the Poor. How do the ideas in these chapters relate to each other?

 C. Review the chapters on Success, Responsible Speech, and Sexuality. How do they derive their values from the ideals of Community and Free Will?

FOR DISCUSSION

 We have studied a full range of Jewish ethical subjects, with their fundamental concern for the individual as well as the community. We can now understand the traditional role of Jews as leaders at the forefront of movements for social welfare and reform.

 The following is an excerpt from a hypothetical ethical will written by an American Jewish activist, Albert Vorspan. Does it conform to the Jewish ethical principles we have studied? Does it go too far? Can one go too far in seeking "to do justice and love mercy?" Discuss your feelings.

 "I leave you . . . (a) title deed which is imbedded in your birthright: to be a Jew is to see the world from a particular angle of vision. To be a Jew is to be mobilized for life in the task of perfecting the world. To take the unfinished world and to shape it on the anvil of life - that is your calling as a Jew. To be unreconciled to the world as it is - that is your charge . . . To be a Jew is to say no when men murmur yes to wrongdoing. To be a Jew is to feel, in the depths of your heart, the pain of your fellow man. To be a Jew is to be discontented with the status quo and unafraid to shake it. To be a Jew is to irritate the conscience of the good, well-intentioned folk who acquiesce in the misery of their fellows. To be a Jew is to get your hands bruised in the arena of action, because a cloistered virtue is un-Jewish, and Jewish belief is tested by deed. To be a Jew is to refuse to surrender to despair . . . To be a Jew is to be as jealous of the rights of the nonconformists, the kooks, the dissenters, the nudniks, as you are of your own. To be a Jew is to be a goad to action. To be a Jew is to be intoxicated with a dream of social justice. It is not easy to be a Jew."